A CENTURY
OF STORIES
NEW HANOVER COUNTY PUBLIC LIBRARY
1906-2006

PACIFIC OCEAN

Jen Green

WORLD ALMANAC® LIBRARY

Please visit our web site at: www.worldalmanaclibrary.com
For a free color catalog describing World Almanac® Library's list of
high-quality books and multimedia programs, call 1-800-848-2928 (USA)
or 1-800-387-3178 (Canada). World Almanac® Library's fax: (414) 332-3567.

Library of Congress Cataloging-in-Publication Data

Green, Jen.
   Pacific Ocean / Jen Green.
      p. cm.—(Oceans and seas)
   Includes bibliographical references and index.
   ISBN 0-8368-6275-9 (lib. bdg.)
   ISBN 0-8368-6283-X (softcover)
    1. Pacific Ocean—Juvenile literature. 1. Title.
  GC771.G73   2006
  551.46'14—dc22   2005054134

First published in 2006 by
World Almanac® Library
A Member of the WRC Media Family of Companies
330 West Olive Street, Suite 100
Milwaukee, WI 53212 USA

Copyright © 2006 by World Almanac® Library.

Produced by Discovery Books
Editor: Sabrina Crewe
Designer and page production: Sabine Beaupré
Photo researcher: Sabrina Crewe
Maps and diagrams: Stefan Chabluk
World Almanac® Library editorial direction: Valerie Weber
World Almanac® Library editor: Gini Holland
World Almanac® Library art direction: Tammy West
World Almanac® Library graphic design: Charlie Dahl
World Almanac® Library production: Jessica Morris and Robert Kraus

Picture credits: Corbis: cover, pp. 18, 19, 36, 38, 39; FLPA: pp. 10, 23 (top), 43; Getty Images:
pp. 13 (top), 16, 20, 23 (bottom), 24 (bottom), 27, 28, 30 (top), 31 (top), 32 (bottom), 33,
40; NOAA: pp. 6, 11, 12, 13 (bottom), 17, 22 (both), 24 (top), 25 (both), 26, 30–31, 32 (top),
35, 37, 41; NOAA/NGDC: title page; USGS: p. 8.

Printed in the United States of America

1 2 3 4 5 6 7 8 9 10 09 08 07 06

CONTENTS

Front cover: *The Pacific Ocean, with its large rolling waves, is popular with surfers. In this photograph, a surfer is riding a wave at Oahu, Hawaii.*
Title page: *This computer-generated image of Earth was based on land and ocean measurements made by the U.S. National Geophysical Data Center. This view shows much of the Pacific Ocean, with the continent of Australia bottom left and North America just visible top right.*

Words that appear in the glossary are printed in **boldface** the first time they occur in text.

It is hard to picture how vast the Pacific Ocean is until one looks at an image of Earth from space. One side of the globe appears to be covered in water—that is the Pacific, the world's largest ocean.

Oldest, Biggest, and Deepest

The Pacific is a record breaker in several other ways, too. It is the world's oldest ocean. At its widest point, between Panama and Malaysia, the Pacific Ocean stretches more than halfway around the world. More than half the world's islands lie in Pacific waters. The Pacific is also the world's deepest ocean. Challenger Deep in the Mariana Trench is the deepest point in all the world's oceans.

Watery World

"Ninety-seven percent of all the water on Earth is in the seas, the greater part of it in the Pacific, which covers half the planet and is bigger than all the landmasses put together. Altogether the Pacific holds over half of all the ocean water."

Bill Bryson, A Short History of Nearly Everything, *2003*

Boundaries of the Pacific Ocean

The Pacific Ocean includes the Bering Sea, the Bering **Strait**, and the **Gulf** of Alaska; the Seas of Okhotsk and Japan; the Gulf of Tonkin; the East and South China Seas; and the Bali, Philippine, Yellow, Arafura, Banda, Celebes, Coral, and Tasman Seas. The Pacific's narrowest point lies in the north. There, the Bering Strait, which is just 53 miles (85 kilometers) wide, leads to the Arctic Ocean. The Pacific is enclosed by the Americas along its eastern shore, merging with the Atlantic Ocean south of **Cape** Horn. To the west lie the continents of Asia and Australia and the islands of Indonesia. South of Australia, Pacific waters mingle with the Indian Ocean. The Southern Ocean and the icy continent of Antarctica lie to the south.

The word *Pacific* means "peaceful." The Pacific, however, is not always peaceful. It can be highly dangerous when storms whip up rough seas or when an earthquake shakes the seabed.

Industry and Shipping

The open waters and surrounding seas of the Pacific are crossed by major shipping routes. Many nations in the region,

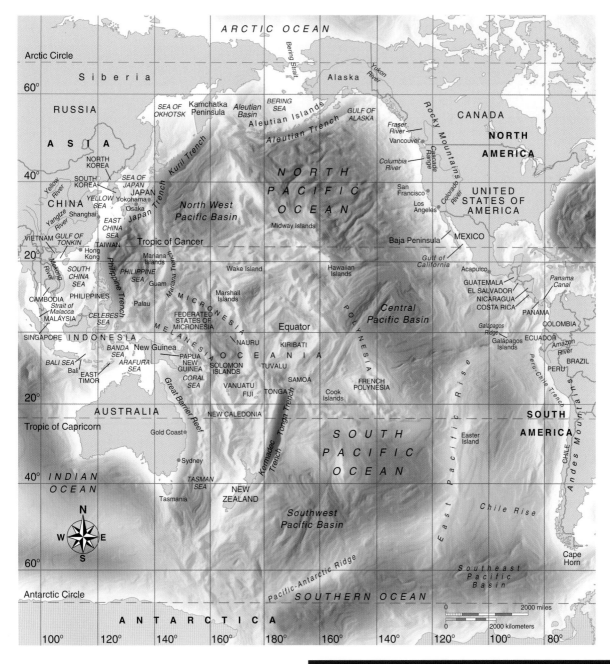

This map shows the Pacific Ocean, its major islands and underwater features, and the landmasses that border it.

including the United States, Japan, and Australia, are highly industrialized. The ocean is rich in resources, which are used by millions of people. The deep, open waters of the Pacific Ocean, however, still hold many mysteries.

Pacific Ocean Key Facts

Surface area: 60,060,700 square miles (155,557,000 square kilometers)

Coastline: 84,301 miles (135,663 km)

Average depth: 13,215 feet (4,028 m)

Deepest known point: 35,840 feet (10,924 m), Challenger Deep in the Mariana Trench

CHAPTER ONE

PHYSICAL FEATURES

More than half of the water in all the world's oceans combined is in the Pacific Ocean. The **equator** divides this vast expanse of water into two roughly equal parts, the North and South Pacific.

The Pacific Ocean floor is extremely uneven, resembling a huge rumpled carpet with long undersea **ridges** and deep furrows, or trenches. In the 1900s, scientists discovered that these features were formed by movements of the giant slabs, called tectonic plates, which make up Earth's outer layers. These movements

Lava from volcanic eruptions can be seen in several forms around the Pacific. This beach in Tahiti is black because the sand is formed from lava.

and other factors ensure that the Pacific Ocean is still changing today.

Formation

Scientists believe the Pacific is Earth's most ancient surviving ocean. The oldest **sediments** found so far, dating back more 135 million years, are located in the western Pacific. Many scientists believe the ocean is even older than that. They trace the ocean's origins to about 200 million years ago, when, they believe, it was formed from Earth's original ocean, Panthalassa.

Spreading Seafloor

Several tectonic plates lie beneath the Pacific. The Pacific Plate, the world's largest plate, underlies the central area. There are several smaller plates on the margins, closer to shore. Scientists have discovered that the Pacific Plate is slowly drifting west, creating a **rift** along its eastern border in a zone called the East Pacific Rise. Molten rock is welling up to fill this gap, forming a long submarine ridge where the seafloor is spreading. The newly erupted **lava** pushes the rocks on either side apart and out toward the edges

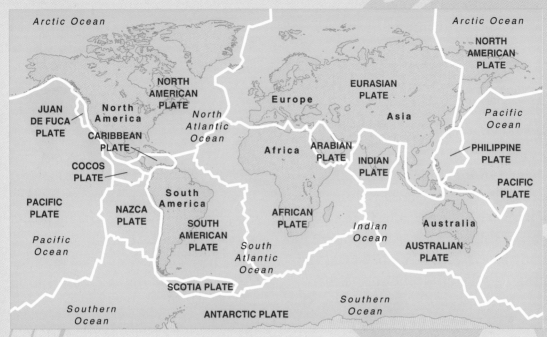

Earth's outer layers are made up of a number of vast, rigid sections called tectonic plates—seven major ones and up to twelve smaller ones. Fitting together like pieces of a jigsaw puzzle, the plates underlie oceans and dry land. The plates drift across Earth's surface, floating on a lower, molten layer of the **mantle** like chunks of bread on a thick, bubbling soup. As they drift, tectonic plates can push together, grind past one another, or pull apart.

Volcanic eruptions and earthquakes are common along plate boundaries because the crust is thinnest there. Where two plates pull apart, as is happening along the East Pacific Rise, **magma** rises to fill the space, creating a mountain chain underwater or on land. Elsewhere, plates collide. When this happens, one plate may dive below the other to form a deep trench, such as the Mariana Trench near the Mariana Islands.

About 250 million years ago, Earth's landmasses were united in a single "supercontinent" named Pangaea, which was surrounded by a vast ocean now known as Panthalassa. About 200 million years ago, because of **continental drift** caused by plate movement, a great bay—the Tethys Sea—opened up in the center of Pangaea and split it in half. The northern landmass—named Laurasia—included North America, Greenland, Europe, and Asia, while the southern half—Gondwanaland—included South America, Africa, India, Australia, and Antarctica. What remained of Panthalassa became the Pacific Ocean. As plate movement continued over millions of years, the continents and oceans took their present positions (shown above, with the major tectonic plates), and they continue to shift today.

of the ocean, where they collide with plates bearing the continents on all sides.

Collision Zones

Where plates collide around the rim of the Pacific, the dense, heavy Pacific Plate is being forced below the lighter continental plates. In these areas, named **subduction zones**, the ocean crust melts and wells up again to form volcanic peaks on land or on the ocean bed. The ring of active volcanoes around the rim of the Pacific that results from this activity is called the Ring of Fire. Plate collision along these borders also causes the continental plates to crumple upward, forming chains of mountains running parallel to the coast. These chains include the Andes in South America and the Cascade Range in North America.

A Shrinking Ocean

Despite the fact that the Pacific floor is spreading in several places, the ocean as a whole is actually shrinking as it is squeezed by the continents on all sides. Until just four million years ago, the Pacific was open to the Atlantic through

The Ring of Fire

The Ring of Fire is a circle of active volcanoes running right around the edge of the Pacific. From Antarctica, the ring curves north through Taupo, New Zealand, and Mount Fuji in Japan to the Aleutian Islands off Alaska. From there, the ring heads south again through the Cascades and Andes back toward Antarctica. Recent eruptions along the Ring of Fire include Mount St. Helens, Washington, in 1980 and Mount Pinatubo in the Philippines in 1991. In 1943, the ring's youngest volcano, Paricutin, erupted in a farmer's field in Mexico and has since grown into a mountain 1,345 feet (410 m) above ground level. Earthquakes are common along the Ring of Fire. In 1964, one of the strongest quakes ever recorded struck the Alaskan coast,

A view of Paricutin volcano, still erupting in 1947. During the first year of eruption in 1943, the cone grew to 1,100 feet (336 m). It continued to grow for another eight years.

sending devastating tsunamis rippling across the ocean. In 1995, Kobe, Japan, was rocked by a violent earthquake that killed 5,400 people.

a passage, the Panama Seaway, between Central and South America. Some 3.5 million years ago, plate movement forced a narrow neck of land, the **isthmus** of Panama, upward to close the gap.

The East Pacific Rise

The floor of the Pacific holds many dramatic features, including mountains higher than Mount Everest and trenches deeper than the Grand Canyon. One of the most important features is the East Pacific Rise, a ridge that runs over 5,400 miles (8,686 km) from west of Mexico to the southern Pacific Ocean. The East Pacific Rise towers about 7,000 feet (2,100 m) above the ocean floor. Along its center is a deep rift valley where newly erupted lava is causing the ocean floor to spread outward at a rate of about 6.5 inches (16.5 centimeters) a year. There are several other volcanic ridges in the Pacific, such as the Chile Rise and Galápagos Ridge off the Americas.

Depths and Shallows

The deepest points in the Pacific are found in its trenches. The Japan, Kuril, and Aleutian Trenches, the Philippine Trench off the Philippines, and the Tonga Trench north of New Zealand are all over 6 miles (10 km) deep. Challenger Deep in the Mariana Trench is easily deep enough to swallow the highest mountains on land.

The western part of the Pacific floor is more uneven and irregular than the eastern region. Much of the north is occupied by a vast, deep plain. Some 18,000 feet (5,500 m) below the surface, this plain covers about 1 million square miles (2.59 million sq km).

All around the Pacific rim, the ocean bed slopes up to the shallow, sloping ledges, called continental shelves, that edge the landmasses of Asia, Australia, and the Americas. The waters of the shelves are mostly less than 600 feet (183 m) deep. The continental shelves

This diagram shows some of the features that form on Earth's ocean floors.

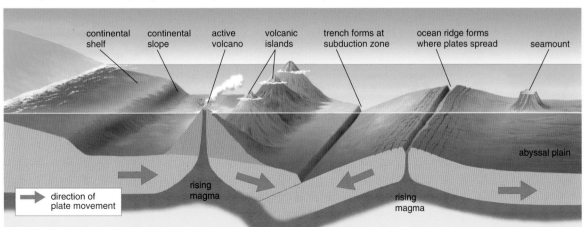

continental shelf — continental slope — active volcano — volcanic islands — trench forms at subduction zone — ocean ridge forms where plates spread — seamount

abyssal plain

→ direction of plate movement

rising magma

rising magma

Hydrothermal Vents

In 1977, scientists exploring the Pacific Ocean depths in **submersibles** made an amazing find. At the Galápagos Ridge off the coast of Ecuador, they discovered extraordinary rock chimneys belching clouds of scalding water, black with the minerals sulfur and iron. These hydrothermal vents, also called "black smokers," are now thought to occur in volcanically active regions in many parts of the oceans. At these sites, ocean water entering cracks in the crust is heated and mixed with newly erupted minerals to gush out again in dark clouds of hot water. The minerals settle and build up around the vents to form chimneys. They also seep out into the ocean, adding to the water's salt levels. "White smokers" have also been found—these vents spew slightly cooler water containing white minerals. Since the first discovery in 1977, several more vents have been discovered in the Pacific, including on the East Pacific Rise.

New Zealand in the South Pacific, like other continental islands, became separated from a larger landmass by plate movements long ago.

of the Americas are fairly narrow. Asia and Australia are edged by wider shelves.

Many Islands

The Pacific Ocean has more than thirty thousand islands. The combined mass of all of the islands in the Pacific, however, occupies less than one percent of the ocean's surface. The largest islands and island groups, such as Japan, New Guinea, and New Zealand, mainly lie near the western rim of the Pacific Ocean. Thousands of small islands dot the western and central areas of the Pacific. This region of small islands is known as Oceania. There are three major island groups in Oceania: Melanesia in the west, Polynesia to the east, and Micronesia north of Melanesia.

Continental Islands

The islands of Pacific can be divided into three main types, which formed in different ways: continental islands, oceanic islands, and coral atolls. Continental islands—such as Japan, New Guinea, and the Philippines—rise from the broad continental shelves along the western rim. Along with New Zealand, these large fragments were once part of neighboring continents.

Oceanic Islands

Out in the open ocean, oceanic islands were formed by volcanic eruptions. Many of these islands lie near subduction zones at plate margins. They formed when lava that had erupted on the ocean floor built up enough to break the water's surface. (Volcanic peaks that remain submerged are named seamounts.) Elsewhere, far from plate margins, some island arcs are located at weak points in the crust near the center of plates. At these sites, known as hot spots, a plume of red-hot magma breaks though the crust, which is slowly drifting over the hot spot. This movement gives rise to a curving chain of islands. The Hawaiian chain contains more than one hundred volcanoes and stretches over 1,700 miles (2,735 km).

Coral Atolls

The third type of island found in the Pacific Ocean is a coral atoll—a hollow ring of coral surrounding a calm **lagoon** in the center. These coral **reefs** originally formed around volcanic islands that later subsided into the sea, leaving just the coral ring. The Pacific holds some of

The islands of Hawaii are volcanic in origin. Mauna Kea on Hawaii is the world's highest mountain, higher than any found on land when measured from Earth's surface. It rises 33,480 feet (10,205 m) from the ocean bed.

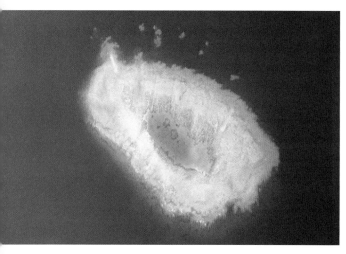

An aerial view of a coral atoll in the western Pacific shows the typical formation of a lagoon of water—usually seawater—surrounded by coral.

The Southern Ocean

The most southern waters of the Pacific Ocean meet those of the Southern Ocean. Until 2000, part of the Southern Ocean was included within the boundaries of the Pacific, but the Southern Ocean was then officially declared separate. The Southern Ocean stretches across 7,848,255 square miles (20,327,000 sq km) of Earth's most southern region, surrounding the icy continent of Antarctica. Much of the ocean is covered by ice in winter. With its strong winds and freezing temperatures, the Southern Ocean is inhospitable to human settlement, but some animals also found in the Pacific, including species of penguins and seals, live there.

the world's largest coral atolls, including Kwajelein in the Marshall Islands and Kiritimati in the Republic of Kiribati.

The Eastern Pacific Coasts

The shores and islands of the Pacific hold a huge variety of coastal scenery, including towering cliffs, rocky headlands, curving bays, and sandy coves. The western edge of the Pacific is much more jagged and indented than the eastern edge, where the shores of the Americas are fairly smooth, with relatively few inlets or promontories. The 750-mile (1,207-km) long Baja **Peninsula**, enclosing the Gulf of California, is a notable exception.

High mountain ranges run right along the American coasts and drop steeply to the water. There is only a narrow coastal plain along these shores. In the far north and south of the Americas, glaciers have carved deep valleys that were later flooded by rising seas to create steep-sided inlets and offshore islands.

Along the Western Pacific

The western coasts of the Pacific are far less regular. Many bays and inlets break up the shorelines, with large peninsulas, such as the Kamchatka and Korean Peninsulas, enclosing fringing seas. Long stretches of coast are backed by broad plains and wide valleys created by mighty rivers, including the Yellow and Yangtze Rivers. These and other rivers that run into the western Pacific flood regularly.

The wide variety of features found on Pacific coasts are shaped by two main processes: erosion and deposition. Erosion is the wearing away of the land by water, wind, and other natural forces. Deposition is the laying down of rocky materials, often in the form of fine particles such as sand, mud, or silt.

A sweeping sandy beach, with just a few rocks not yet worn away by waves, curves along the Pacific Ocean's eastern shore at Cayucos, California (top). High ground forms a very different type of coastline at Molokai, Hawaii (bottom), where towering cliffs rise from the ocean.

Waves are the main force of erosion on coastlines. As they beat against the shore, they hurl sand and **shingle** against rocks to wear them away. Bands of hard rock at the water's edge are left to form jutting headlands, while soft rocks are eaten away to form deep, curving bays. High ground near the shore is undercut to form steep cliffs. Molokai in Hawaii has the world's highest cliffs, towering over 0.6 miles (1 km) high.

Out to sea, the pounding waves smash rocky fragments into sand and shingle. Coastal **currents** may carry these materials for miles along the shore and then deposit them to form **barrier islands,** beaches, and **spits.** Elsewhere, at river mouths, sediment carried toward the ocean by rivers is dropped to form flat, swampy **deltas,** such as the Mekong Delta. The silt dropped by China's Yellow River has joined what was a large island in the river's mouth onto the mainland, creating the Shandong Peninsula.

CHAPTER TWO

CLIMATE AND CURRENTS

All the water in the Pacific is not the same. Temperatures, **salinity**, and oxygen levels vary in different parts of the ocean and at various depths. The North Pacific is fed by many large rivers, including the Yukon, Fraser, Columbia, and Colorado Rivers in North America, and the Yellow, Yangtze, and Mekong in Asia. Less fresh water drains into the South Pacific from the rivers of South America and Australia because the climate is drier there.

Why Is the Ocean Salty?

Ocean water is salty because it contains dissolved minerals, or salts, washed from the land by rivers or released underwater from hydrothermal vents and volcanic eruptions. The salt level in ocean water is higher than in rivers because, when surface water **evaporates**, the dissolved salts remain in the oceans and become more concentrated. Experts calculate that the salt in all the seas and oceans would be enough to bury Earth's landmasses to a depth of 500 feet (152 m)! So why don't oceans and seas get increasingly salty as new minerals are added each year? Some salt is removed from the water when it is absorbed by marine life or reacts with underwater rock and eventually forms new sediment layers on the sea floor. These processes help keep salt levels constant in the oceans.

Water Temperatures

The temperature of surface waters varies with climate in different parts of the Pacific Ocean. In the **Tropics**, surface temperatures can rise to 90° Fahrenheit (32° Celsius) and remain warm all year round. Water temperatures may drop as low as 28° F (-2° C) in the far north and far south of the Pacific in winter. In the central Pacific, surface temperatures are also affected by the recurring changes of an ocean pattern called El Niño.

Pacific Winds

Four great belts of wind blow at different **latitudes** in the Pacific. Winds are named after the direction from which they blow. Steady easterly winds, called trade winds, blow toward the equator from the **subtropical** regions. At the equator itself, a belt of light winds, known as the doldrums, often stalls sailboats. North and south of the trade wind belt, westerly **prevailing winds** blow between latitudes 30° and 60°. These winds vary more than the trade winds. The most powerful winds of the region are associated with the giant revolving storms called **tropical** cyclones, which form in some regions of the Pacific Ocean in summer and fall.

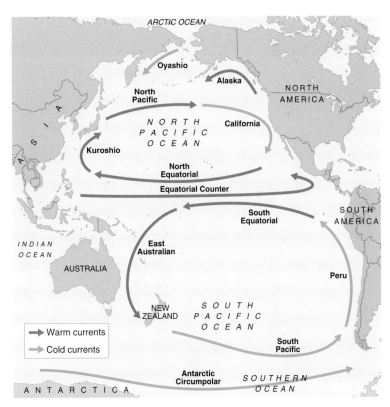

This map shows the most important surface currents found in the Pacific Ocean.

Pacific Currents

Prevailing winds blowing across the Pacific Ocean create surface currents and cause the water to flow around in giant circles named **gyres**. In the North Pacific, the main flow is clockwise. The North Equatorial Current carries water west above the equator. The flow then heads north as the warm Kuroshio Current, east as the North Pacific Current, and finally south again as the cold California Current, to complete the gyre. Other currents circulate in the far north of the ocean.

In the South Pacific, another gyre flows counterclockwise. It involves the westward-flowing South Equatorial Current, the southward-moving East Australian Current, the eastward-flowing South Pacific, and the cold Peru Current, which carries water north

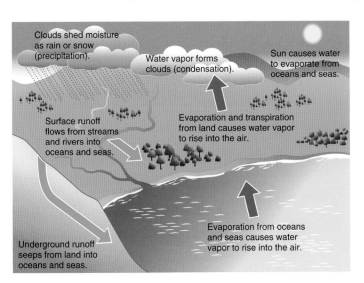

Moisture continually circulates between the oceans, air, and land. This never-ending process, illustrated here, is known as the water cycle.

Every three to seven years, a climate change takes place in the Pacific Ocean. A large mass of warm water, usually located near Australia, shifts east toward South America. At the same time, trade winds weaken. This altered pattern is known as El Niño, and there are a number of theories about why it happens. What is certain is that El Niño has several impacts on the region. When El Niño warms the cold waters off South America, it causes stocks of fish and seabirds to fall. The unusual warming of these waters also brings heavy rains and sometimes flooding to South America. Australia, Asia, and even distant Africa, on the other hand, can be hit by droughts. El Niño lasts for a year or more. The

A rancher examines dead livestock on his cattle station in Australia during a 2005 drought caused by El Niño weather patterns.

ocean then reverts to its normal patterns, or sometimes a reverse event called La Niña occurs. During La Niña, waters in the eastern Pacific become unusually cold. La Niña can also bring climate changes that are the opposite to those of El Niño.

up the South American coast. At the equator, the Equatorial Countercurrent returns water eastward. In 1992, the accidental spill of thousands of rubber ducks helped scientists study Pacific currents! Scientists tracked water flow by observing where the little ducks washed up.

Water circulates in the ocean depths as well as near the surface. Deepwater currents are driven mainly by differences in temperature and salinity between various water masses. The West Wind Drift off Antarctica helps to mix bottom waters. Deep, mineral-rich water rises in **upwellings** off the coast of Peru and makes this region rich in marine life.

Powerful Waves

The Pacific Ocean does not always live up to its peaceful name. Many of the world's most powerful waves have occurred in Pacific waters. A towering 111-foot (34-m) wave, recorded there in 1933, holds the record for the world's highest natural wave.

As waves sweep across the ocean, the water in them moves around in a circle. Out to sea, the water is able to circulate freely. Near coasts, however, reefs or the ocean bed hinder the flow of water. The wave slows down and rears up to form a foaming crest that crashes on the shore. The waves pounding the northeast coast of Maui, Hawaii, are among the world's tallest breakers. Along one stretch of coast there, waves regularly reach 50 to 60 feet (15 to 18 m) high. Daring sailboarders and surfers travel to Hawaii to ride these famous waves.

Tsunamis

Huge waves called tsunamis can occur when earthquakes, volcanic eruptions, or landslides shake the ocean floor. The waves radiate outward from the center of disturbance like giant ripples, racing across the ocean at up to 470 miles (756 km) per hour. At such speeds, a tsunami takes just five hours to cover the huge distance between the Aleutian Islands and Hawaii.

In 1883, the eruption of the Krakatoa volcano in Indonesia sent tsunamis racing across the Pacific Ocean. More than one hundred coastal settlements were destroyed, and about thirty-six thousand people died. In 1960, a violent earthquake off the coast of Chile raised huge waves that swamped several Chilean cities, killing one thousand people. The tsunamis went on to cause more death and destruction on the coasts of Japan, California, and Hawaii.

Climate

From the Bering Strait in the far north to Cape Horn in the south, the climate of the Pacific varies from subpolar to tropical and back again. The far north

---

A tsunami sweeps over a pier as it hits the shore at Hilo, Hawaii, in 1946. This devastating wave prompted the United States to establish a tsunami warning system in the islands. Hawaii was at the time a U.S. territory.

A cruise ship passes an iceberg in the freezing waters of southern Chile. The extreme north and south of the Pacific Ocean are close to polar regions, and the climate is very different from that in the tropical center of the ocean.

is somewhat warmer than the far south because the northern ocean is largely enclosed by landmasses of Asia and North America. The northern region, however, still has long, cold winters and short, cool summers. In the central North Pacific, the climate is stormy and unpredictable. The central South Pacific has

What Causes Tides?

Tides are regular rises and falls in sea level caused mainly by the tug of the Moon's gravity. As the Moon orbits Earth, its gravity pulls ocean water into a mound below it. A similar bulge appears on the ocean on the opposite side of Earth because the planet itself is also being pulled, by the same force, away from the water on the far side. As Earth spins eastward, so the mounds move westward across Earth's surface, bringing tides to coasts in succession. Because Earth spins around once every twenty-four hours, the two bulges both move across Earth once in that period, creating two tides a day in each place. The tides are not always equal in volume, however. In some parts of more enclosed bodies of water, such as the South China Sea, there is just one tide a day.

The Sun's gravity exerts a similar, but weaker, pull on the oceans. This is because while many times larger than the Moon, it is also much farther away. Every two weeks, at the full moon and again during the new moon, the Sun and Moon line up so that their pulls combine. This force brings extra high tides called spring tides. They alternate with weaker tides also occurring every two weeks, named neap tides, when the two pulls tend to minimize each other. Tides are generally high on Pacific coasts. The ocean's highest tides occur off the west coast of Korea, where the water rises and falls by up to 29 feet (8.8 m).

mild summers, cool winters, and abundant rainfall brought by tropical storms.

Pacific Cyclones

Tropical cyclones form in the trade wind belt in late summer and early fall, becoming huge revolving storms that can measure hundreds of miles across and cause enormous damage. They begin far out in the ocean, at centers of **low pressure** where warm, moist air is rising upward. As the rising air cools, its moisture **condenses**, bringing lashing rain and releasing heat that fuels the developing storm. Winds then spiral faster and faster around the center of low pressure, which becomes the calm "eye" in the center of the cyclone. Large tropical cyclones are called hurricanes in the eastern Pacific, typhoons in the northwest Pacific, and severe tropical cyclones in the southwest Pacific.

Many cyclones blow out in the open ocean without causing much damage, but some sweep northwest to menace the coasts of the Philippines, Japan, and China. The largest and strongest cyclone ever recorded was the 1979 Typhoon Tip in the northwest Pacific. Hurricane Iniki in 1992 was the worst cyclone on record in Hawaii. Recent years have seen some severe cyclones in the Pacific Ocean, including Typhoon Tokage of 2004, Japan's worst storm in twenty-five years.

Cyclones can create another danger. The fierce winds around the cyclone's eye cause seawater to pile up and form a mound of water called a storm surge. The effect is similar to a tsunami when the water reaches land.

In 1991, Typhoon Thelma devastated the island of Leyte in the Philippines. About six thousand people were killed in the resulting landslides and floods.

CHAPTER THREE

MARINE LIFE

The Pacific has the greatest variety of living things found in any ocean, including many of the very largest and smallest species. The long list of species includes many that are endemic, or found only in these waters. Some Pacific creatures are related to Indian Ocean species—and, to a lesser extent, Atlantic species—because the waters of the Pacific mingle in places with the other two oceans.

Coastal Habitats

Coastal Pacific waters hold a wide variety of **habitats**. In warm, tropical waters, mangrove swamps and sea-grass beds shelter fish, shellfish, and turtles. In colder inshore waters off the Americas, kelp beds form undersea forests, where the giant seaweed sways in the currents. Seabirds and shorebirds nest on cliffs, mudflats, beaches, and deltas.

The Great Barrier Reef is the world's largest coral reef, stretching 1,250 miles (2,011 km) along the northeastern coast of Australia. Reefs such as the Great Barrier Reef are thousands or even millions of years old.

Coral Reefs

Coral reefs are the ocean's richest habitat. They form in warm, shallow waters in the tropical and subtropical areas. These hard structures are built by small creatures called coral **polyps** that attach to firm surfaces, such as rocks or the reef itself. Coral polyps use minerals dissolved in seawater to build a protective, chalky skeleton around their soft bodies. When they die, their cup-shaped skeletons remain and slowly build up on top of others to form a rocky reef. Some coral formations resemble plants; others look like rocks or plates. The polyps catch food with their tentacles and are also nourished by **algae** that live inside them.

The Great Barrier Reef off the coast of northeastern Australia is home to over 3,000 species, including some 300 different types of coral and about 1,500 species of fish. Many reef fish have striped or spotted markings that camouflage them them on the coral reefs.

Ocean Food Chains

In the Pacific as in other oceans, living things depend on one another for food. The relationships between plants and animals in a habitat can be shown in a food chain. Plants form the base of almost all marine food chains. Seaweeds and tiny floating plants, or phytoplankton, use light to make their food through the process of **photosynthesis**. Tiny animals called zooplankton feed on the plants. Off the coast of Peru, small fish named anchoveta feed on the **plankton**. They are snapped up by larger fish, such as tuna or bonito, which in turn may be caught by sharks or people. When living things die, their remains are eaten by scavengers and broken down by bacteria, which helps to recycle the energy their bodies contain.

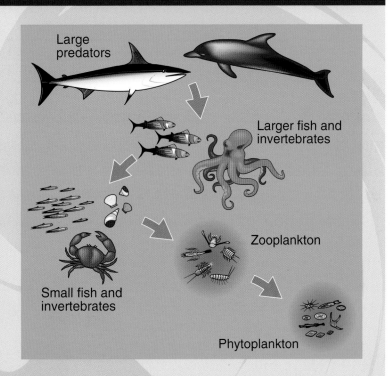

Large predators

Larger fish and invertebrates

Zooplankton

Small fish and invertebrates

Phytoplankton

Island Evolution

The islands of the Pacific hold many
unique creatures. The Hawaiian islands
have several colorful birds called honey-
creepers. The Galápagos Islands off
Ecuador are home to all sorts of unusual
animals, including giant tortoises,
marine iguanas, and about a dozen types
of finch. On a visit to the Galápagos in
1835, British naturalist Charles Darwin
noticed that each island had its own
variety of finch, closely related to—but
not the same as—species on other islands.
Darwin believed that all the finches were
descended from a single species that had
reached the islands long ago. The dozen
or so varieties had then **evolved** to suit
conditions found on particular islands.
Darwin's visit to the islands helped him
develop the theory of evolution.

A purple-striped jellyfish (top) floats in the euphotic zone.

Open Waters

Out in the open ocean, marine life is
most abundant in the sunlit upper water,
or **euphotic zone**, which extends from
the surface down to 330–660 feet
(100–200 m). Plants, such as seaweeds
and tiny algae, thrive here, providing
food for creatures such as jellyfish,
shrimp, and surface-dwelling fish.

The mid-depths, or **bathyal zone**,
between 330–660 feet and 6,600 feet

Discovery in the Deep

When scientists discovered hydrothermal
vents in the Pacific Ocean, they were
astonished to find communities of unique
creatures living there. Hydrothermal vent
species include tube worms (*shown right*),
blind crabs, clams, sea anemones, and tiny
fish. Unlike almost all other living things
in the sea or on land, these animals do
not depend on the sunlight and oxygen of
typical food chains, living instead on the
bacteria that thrive in the hot, mineral-
rich water gushing from the vents. Some
vent species, such as alvinellid worms, are
able to tolerate both the scorching heat
of the vent and the extreme cold of the
surrounding deep waters.

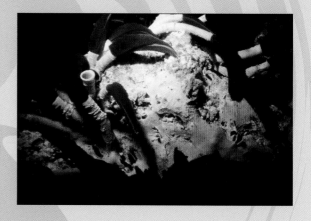

A giant kelp forest flourishes in Pacific waters off the coast of California.

(100–200 m and 2,000 m) contain fewer creatures because plants cannot grow in the gloomy water that receives only glimmers of light from above. Marine life is even more scarce in the inky-black waters of the **abyssal zone** below 6,600 feet (2,000 m). Creatures here must be able to withstand enormous pressure as well as extreme cold and lack of light. Gulper eels and deep-sea anglerfish have huge mouths and stretchy stomachs so they can snap up any prey they come across. Despite the scarcity of deepwater species, the depths of the Pacific are still home to more animals than any other part of the ocean because of the huge volume of water there.

Plants in the Pacific

Plants of the Pacific range in size from microscopic plankton to giant kelp. The plankton bloom, or multiply, quickly in northern and southern Pacific waters in summer. Marine animals—from small fish to giant whales—travel to these waters to feast on the seasonal abundance. Off the rocky coasts of North America, beds of brown kelp flourish. The world's largest seaweed, brown kelp has fronds up to 100 feet (30 m) long.

Invertebrates

The majority of animals living in Pacific waters are invertebrates—creatures that lack an inner skeleton. Invertebrates include **mollusks**, crabs, lobsters, sea urchins, corals, starfish, jellyfish, and sponges. Many invertebrates dwell on the ocean floor, but octopus, squid, and cuttlefish are free swimmers. Mollusks of the Pacific include some of the world's

Humboldt squid, like this one off the coast of Mexico, can grow up to 6 feet (2 m) long and weigh 100 pounds (45 kilograms). These mollusks live only in the eastern Pacific, where they hunt for smaller mollusks and fish and are hunted in turn by whales, large fish, and people.

A marine iguana approaches a resting sea lion in the Galápagos Islands in the eastern Pacific.

largest species: the giant squid of deep waters and the Pacific giant clam that inhabits coral reefs.

Fish and Reptiles

The Pacific contains about half of all fish species, ranging in size from tiny reef fish to huge whale sharks. Anchovetas, sardines, and flying fish are among the species that swim at the surface, while hake and pollack skim along the ocean bed. Six types of tuna found in the Pacific include yellowfin tuna, which swim with dolphins, and albacore, which are known to **migrate** up to 5,300 miles (8,527 km) from Japan to California. There are also six species of salmon that migrate long distances. These fish mature in the streams of Asia and North America and then move to the open ocean. After spending up to five years in the North Pacific, they return to the rivers where they hatched to lay their own eggs.

Pacific reptiles include several types of sea turtles, including leatherbacks, the world's largest turtle. The Indo-Pacific crocodile, which lurks in swamps of the western Pacific from the Philippines south to Australia, is the biggest crocodile. Marine iguanas of the Galápagos Islands are the world's only seagoing lizards. These reptiles dive off the islands' shores to graze on seaweed. Several small islands off New Zealand are home to the tuatara, a unique reptile that resembles a lizard but is classed in a group of its own.

Birds of the Pacific

Terns and shearwaters are among bird species that undertake long migrations

Pacific salmon migrate in large groups—these salmon off the Kamchatka Peninsula in Russia are heading for their spawning grounds.

Humpback whales surface in Pacific waters near Hawaii. This kind of vertical surfacing is called spyhopping.

across the Pacific Ocean between their feeding and breeding grounds. Albatross spend almost all their lives on the wing. Cormorants and boobies catch fish by plunge-diving into the water. Boobies are known for the comical, dancelike displays with which they attract their partners.

Pacific islands are home to several unique birds, some of which cannot fly. New Zealand has several flightless species, including the kiwi—with its hair-like feathers—the rare takahe, and the kakapo, a nonflying parrot.

Marine Mammals

Several members of the seal family live in and around the Pacific Ocean, including fur seals, sea lions, and walruses, which bask on rocky coasts in the north. Toothed whales range in size from the Gulf porpoise, just 5 feet (1.5 m) long, to the huge sperm whale. Baleen whales include bowheads, gray whales, and humpbacks. Gray whales travel on long migrations, swimming 12,400 miles (19,950 km) from their feeding grounds in Alaska to breed off the Mexican coast.

Southern Sea Otters

Southern sea otters live in the coastal waters of the northern Pacific. Sea otters have the thickest fur of any animal, made of two layers with up to one million hairs per square inch! The otter's coat has pockets made by skin flaps under its front legs where it stashes its prey. Otters are one of the very few mammals known to use tools. After gathering shellfish on the ocean floor, they float on their backs at the water's surface and crack or pry the shells open using a rock. Otters rest in kelp forests along the Pacific coast, draping the kelp over their bodies to act as an anchor while they sleep.

CHAPTER FOUR

PEOPLE AND SETTLEMENT

Since ancient times, the coasts of the Pacific have offered foods such as fish and shellfish, fertile soil for farming, and a means of transportation. The coasts of the northwest Pacific were the first part of the region to be settled by humans.

Early Human Movements

Scientists believe that humans were living on the shores of eastern Asia as long ago as 90,000 B.C. and had spread to Southeast Asia by 60,000 B.C. At this time, sea levels were lower than they are today. Pacific islands were therefore

bigger, and land stretched much of the way south from Southeast Asia through Indonesia and New Guinea to Australia. Early humans used these land bridges to reach and settle New Guinea and Australia some time about 50,000 B.C.

At least fifteen thousand years ago, and maybe well before, people reached the Americas from Asia. Ancient human footprints, embedded in volcanic ash, were identified in Mexico in 2005. Scientific dating of the prints indicates that people may have reached Mexico by about thirty-eight thousand years ago, long before previous estimates. Humans eventually spread to all parts of the Americas.

Life on Pacific Coasts

The first inhabitants of Pacific coasts probably lived a wandering lifestyle, fishing, hunting wild animals, and gathering

A traditional home on Yap in the Caroline Islands of Micronesia displays money stones to indicate wealth. The stones were mined in limestone caves on Palau, 300 miles (480 km) away, and transported by canoe.

wild foods. In the cold far north, Native peoples hunted whales and seals. Later, when people learned how to grow crops, many central coastal areas offered rich soil and a mild, sunny climate that favored cultivation. Farming began along the rivers of China leading to the Pacific as early as 5000 B.C. By about 2500 B.C., groups in Central and South America, Vietnam, Indonesia, and New Guinea were raising crops.

Civilizations of ancient times included the Chinese and Japanese, both several thousand years old. The Maya civilization of Mexico and Central America lasted from about 500 B.C. to A.D. 900. Much later, in the South American Andes, the Inca developed an advanced culture that lasted from A.D. 1100s through the 1500s.

Settling the Islands

The first people to use boats in Pacific waters were probably the ancestors of modern islanders in Oceania. About 2000 B.C., the coastal peoples of Southeast Asia began to venture across the ocean in search of new areas to settle—possibly because their own lands were crowded and local forests had been mostly cut down. Traveling in canoes with woven straw sails, these groups took animals, plants and seeds for crops, and tools to work the soil.

The islands of Melanesia, in the west, were settled first. From there, islanders gradually spread north to Micronesia and east to Polynesia, reaching the remote

Easter Island Statues

Easter Island is about 2,300 miles (3,700 km) west of South America and 1,130 miles (1,820 km) east of Pitcairn Island—a long way from anywhere by canoe. On the island, there are nearly nine hundred huge statues—up to 40 feet (12 m) tall—made of hardened volcanic ash. The statues, called "moai," were probably carved between A.D. 1400 and 1600 by a people called the Rappa Nui, who have since died out. Archaeologists believe they represent ancestral spirits.

Easter Island by 500 B.C. These long, dangerous voyages must have taken courage and great skill at **navigation**.

By A.D. 800, a Polynesian people called the Maori had reached Aotearoa, or the islands of New Zealand. There, they lived by hunting seals and giant flightless birds and by gathering shellfish.

New Arrivals

In the 1500s, Europeans reached the Pacific Ocean and soon began to influence the way of life there. In 1520–1521, Portuguese navigator Ferdinand Magellan sailed right across the Pacific. Dutch explorers Willem Jansz and Abel Tasman followed in the 1600s, becoming the first Europeans to reach Australia and New Zealand. In the 1700s, Russian, French, and British explorers—including Captain James Cook of Britain—charted the

European colonists came to exploit the resources of the Pacific islands and coasts. They set up plantations, such as this sugarcane plantation in Hawaii.

remote waters of the Pacific and visited many islands.

European settlers soon followed the first explorers. They set up **colonies** and trading posts and began to exploit the riches of the region. Luxuries, such as silk and spices, were shipped from China and Southeast Asia, while coconut oil and sandalwood traveled from Pacific islands. In the north, meanwhile, Russians had colonized coastal Siberia. In the 1700s to 1800s, they established settlements on the Pacific coasts of Alaska and Canada and even as far south as California.

Colonies and Independence

By the 1700s, Europeans had colonized lands right around the rim of the Pacific Ocean. The original inhabitants were often treated badly by the newcomers, either enslaved or forced to work in harsh conditions. Many islanders died of diseases brought by the Europeans, to which they had no natural immunity.

By the end of the 1800s, the coastal nations of the Americas had gained independence from Europe. Australia and New Zealand followed suit in 1907, but most Pacific islands remained in the hands of European nations for at least another fifty years. The United States, a nation itself formed from colonies, claimed islands such as Hawaii, the Philippines, and Guam.

Island Nations

During the second half of the twentieth century, many islands finally gained independence or self-government. Today, there are about a dozen independent island nations in the Pacific, including Fiji, the Solomons, Vanuatu, Tonga, Western Samoa, and Kiribati. Island nations range in size from Papua New Guinea, covering about 178,000 square miles (460,000 sq km), to the tiny island state of Nauru, just 8 square miles (21 sq km) in size.

Some island groups retain strong links with other nations. New Caledonia, for example, is still part of France. Hawaii became the fiftieth U.S. state in 1959. Colonial influence lives on in the customs, religion, architecture, and sometimes languages of many islands. These small, scattered island groups are, however, amazingly diverse in terms of Native culture. One-third of the world's languages are spoken in just four places: Papua New Guinea, the Solomon Islands, Vanuatu, and New Caledonia.

Military Importance

The islands, coasts, and waters of the Pacific have held strategic importance as far back as the 1500s, when Spanish galleons carrying gold and riches from Spain's colonies were attacked by the ships of rival nations. U.S. interest in the region dates to the 1800s, when the U.S. Navy began to patrol Pacific waters and, like other nations, set up military bases on various islands. Today, U.S. bases on Wake and Midway occupy almost all of those small islands.

During the early 1900s, Japan began to carve out an empire in the Pacific. Between 1930 and 1942, Japanese forces occupied many islands in the south and west. During World War II, Japan fought on the side of Germany.

In 1941, the United States entered the war on the side of the Allies after Japan attacked its military base at Pearl Harbor, Hawaii. In 1945, the United States forced Japan's surrender by dropping a devastating new weapon, the atomic bomb, on the cities of Hiroshima and Nagasaki. The United States, Britain, and France have

During the 1800s, large populations and many industries developed around the busiest ports of the Pacific Ocean, transforming them into major cities. Today, the business district of Sydney, Australia, still centers on the harbor, shown here.

since carried out tests of other nuclear weapons at various sites in the Pacific.

Growth of Ports and Industry

From early times, settlements and ports grew up on Pacific coasts and islands where bays and inlets offered shelter for ships. In the western Pacific, the ports of China, Japan, and other Asian countries date back to medieval times and beyond. In the eastern Pacific, ports including San Francisco and Acapulco, Mexico, date to the days of European colonization and settlement.

In the 1800s, Australia, the United States, and New Zealand were among the first Pacific nations to become industrialized. Los Angeles and Sydney, Australia, became centers of manufacturing,

processing raw materials that arrived from abroad. After World War II, Japan industrialized rapidly. In the 1980s and 1990s, Taiwan, Singapore, South Korea, Indonesia, Malaysia, China, and the Philippines followed suit. Today, the United States and Japan are the world's top manufacturing nations, with China catching up fast. Great ports of the Pacific Ocean now include Singapore, Yokohama in Japan, Hong Kong in China, and Kaohsiung in Taiwan.

Ways of Life

Ways of life vary greatly in different parts of the Pacific. As well as highly industrialized nations with modern, high-rise cities, there are also less developed regions. These regions include some small island nations, where most people live in ways that have changed little for centuries: fishing, growing fruit and vegetables, and rearing a few poultry and pigs.

All across the Pacific region, in both developed and developing nations, many people still depend on the ocean for their living. They fish, work in the region's mines and factories, grow crops, or work in the tourist business. Despite regional hazards, such as cyclones, volcanoes, and earthquakes, many coasts and islands are now densely populated. The nations of the western Pacific hold one-third of all the people on Earth.

In Asia, traditional Pacific culture coexists with the modern world. These workers in Taiwan, a heavily populated and industrialized nation, still harvest milkfish in coastal ponds as the Taiwanese people have done for at least four hundred years.

San Francisco

In 1776, the small settlement of Yerba Buena, California, grew up around the Spanish mission of San Francisco de Asís. The town grew slowly at first, having just one hundred inhabitants when California was ceded by Mexico to become part of the United States in 1846. Yerba Buena was renamed San Francisco in 1847. When the gold rush began in California in 1849, the city's population jumped to ten thousand as people arrived from all around the world. By 1870, San Francisco had become the tenth-largest U.S. city. In 1906, seven hundred people died when a major earthquake rocked the city, sparking fires that destroyed many buildings. Modern buildings are built to withstand earthquakes, which are a constant risk in a city built on the notorious San Andreas Fault. San Francisco is now a major center for industry and business as well as a thriving port. It has a large Asian population, an indication of how migration has connected the peoples of the Pacific.

CHAPTER FIVE

TRANSPORTATION AND COMMUNICATION

The first seafarers of the Pacific, the Polynesians, set out across the ocean in two types of vessels: canoes with two **hulls** joined by a platform, like a catamaran; and single-hulled canoes balanced by a floating **outrigger**.

Changes in Shipping

Chinese junks were the most impressive ships of medieval times. These massive wooden vessels had as many as five or six masts with huge sails—often made of bamboo—and watertight compartments below deck. Italian traveler Marco Polo admired the vessels when he visited China in the 1200s: "Most have at least sixty cabins, each of which can comfortably accommodate a merchant," he wrote.

Between the 1500s and 1700s, the multimasted sailing ships of European nations dominated the oceans. After the mid-1800s, steam-powered engines

In the Caroline Islands, (top), people still travel long distances in outrigger canoes. A Chinese junk (bottom) floats in Hong Kong Harbor.

began to replace sails as a means of propulsion. A wide variety of vessels now travel Pacific waters, from traditional canoes and fishing boats to fast motor boats, ferries, and cruise liners to huge **container** ships and oil **tankers**.

Communications Systems

In the Pacific Ocean, ships' crews keep in regular contact with ports, weather stations, and other vessels by radio. The development of **satellite** phones and radios offers instant communication right across the vast distances of the Pacific.

During the late 1900s, Pacific Ocean nations set up tsunami warning systems to reduce the number of deaths caused by these huge waves. Instruments called seismometers have been set up on coasts to detect the earthquakes that cause most

Navigating the Pacific Ocean

Polynesian sailors used the position of stars, the shapes of clouds, the routes of migrating birds, and *te lapa*—rays or lines of light in the water—to find their way across the Pacific Ocean. They recorded their epic journeys on complex charts made by stringing shells, representing reefs and islands, onto strips of cane. Early European sailors, such as Ferdinand Magellan, navigated using magnetic compasses devised in the 1200s. They also used instruments such as cross staffs—which measured the height of the Sun, Moon, and stars above the horizon— to calculate latitude. The chronometer was needed to calculate **longitude**. British explorer Captain James Cook tested the first successful marine chronometer, made by John Harrison, on his long ocean voyages. Modern ships are equipped with a range of sophisticated instruments that allow sailors to chart their position and locate hazards, such as reefs and shallows.

These sailboats are in a world championship competition near the coast of California. Sailors navigate huge distances of the Pacific Ocean during some races.

These systems include **sonar** and **radar**. Gyrocompasses and global positioning systems (GPS) now allow ships to pinpoint their position using satellites.

tsunamis. When one of these instruments detects a quake, scientists issue warnings to coastal settlements.

Freight on the Pacific

The first cargoes to travel the Pacific were the livestock, seeds and plants, and farm tools carried by the Polynesians on their pioneering voyages. From the late 1400s, European vessels, laden with Asian silks and spices or gold from the Americas, crossed the Pacific to return to Europe.

Airplanes are now used to transport many types of **freight**, but bulky and heavy cargoes, such as minerals and vehicles, still go by sea. Today, one of the most valuable cargoes to travel the Pacific

The Panama Canal

Before 1900, all ships traveling between the Pacific and Atlantic Oceans had to go by way of Cape Horn, at the southern tip of South America. In 1914, the Panama Canal opened across the narrow isthmus of Panama. The Canal shortened the journey between the Atlantic and Pacific by several thousand miles. The canal has six pairs of locks that raise and lower the water level as ships cross the high ground of the isthmus. The 50-mile (80-km) journey from one end of the canal to the other takes about eight hours, and thousands of vessels use the canal every year.

Ocean is oil. In general, most raw materials pass from east to west and from south to north, while manufactured goods travel in the opposite directions.

Shipping Routes

Pacific waters contain some of the world's most heavily used shipping lanes. Major routes link Singapore, Japan, and China with Australia and North America.

Two narrow channels are especially busy. The Strait of Malacca between Malaysia and Indonesia connects the Pacific with the Indian Ocean. The Panama Canal across Central America links the Pacific to the Atlantic. The volume of freight crossing the ocean has increased steadily as Asian nations on the Pacific coast have become industrialized. Today, the merchant fleets of China, Japan, South Korea, and the Philippines are among the world's largest.

Pacific Dangers

Hazards for shipping in Pacific waters include storms, cyclones, reefs in the Tropics, ice in the far north and south, **shoals**, and fog. In addition, pirates have operated in the ocean since colonial times, when Spanish treasure ships sailing from Acapulco, Mexico, to the Philippines were regularly attacked. Over the centuries, many valuable cargoes have been lost. A highlight of recent **salvage** operations was the recovery in 1991 of eight hundred pieces of priceless Chinese porcelain from the Spanish ship *San Diego*,

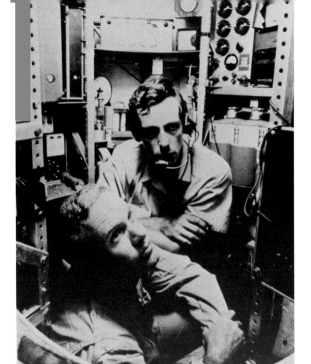

Swiss scientist Jacques Piccard (above) and U.S. Navy lieutenant Don Walsh descend in the U.S. Navy bathyscaphe Trieste *to the bottom of the Mariana Trench. The craft was built by Piccard's father Auguste, a pioneering inventor and explorer.*

which had been sunk by Dutch pirates off the Philippines in 1600. Piracy is still a danger in Southeast Asian waters, including in the Strait of Malacca.

Undersea Exploration

The first ship to investigate the depths of the Pacific was the British research vessel HMS *Challenger*. On a voyage around the world in 1874–1875, the ship's crew took ocean floor samples and brought creatures up from the depths. In 1960, Swiss oceanographer Jacques Piccard and Don Walsh of the U.S. Navy descended to Earth's deepest point, Challenger Deep in the Mariana Trench off the Mariana Islands, in a type of submersible named a bathyscaphe. In 1977, the U.S. research

submersible *Alvin* discovered the first hydrothermal vent at the Galápagos Ridge off South America.

Today, underwater surveys are largely carried out by drilling ships, sonar, satellites, and unmanned submersibles. In 1996, the remotely operated *Kaiko* explored Challenger Deep. A recent satellite study suggests that the ocean floor is subducting faster along the Pacific's Kermadec and Tonga Trenches than at any other site in the oceans.

Life in the Greatest Depths

"Indifferent to the nearly 200,000 tons of pressure clamped on her metal sphere, the *Trieste* balanced herself delicately on the few pounds of guide rope that lay on the bottom, making token claim, in the name of science and humanity, to the ultimate depths in all our oceans—the Challenger Deep. . . . Lying on the bottom just beneath us was some type of flatfish, resembling a sole, about one foot long and six inches across. Even as I saw him, his two round eyes on top of his head spied us—a monster of steel—invading his silent realm. . . . Here, in an instant, was the answer that biologists had asked for the decades. Could life exist in the greatest depths of the ocean? It could!"

Jacques Piccard, Seven Miles Down: The Story of the Bathyscaph Trieste, *1961*

CHAPTER SIX

RESOURCES

The natural resources of the Pacific Ocean, such as fish and minerals, are an important part of life for many people who live in and around the ocean. The region is vast, however, and its diverse economy depends on other resources, including its huge coastal populations.

Nations of the Pacific Rim

There is a marked contrast between the small islands found within Pacific waters and the powerful nations that border the ocean. These nations, several of them large and heavily populated, are collectively known as the "Pacific Rim." China,

Factories and processing plants dominate many coasts in Pacific Rim nations. This photo shows an industrial area on the shore of the Pacific Ocean at Kawasaki, Japan.

Japan, Australia, Canada, and the United States are all economic giants along the Pacific Rim. Other Pacific Rim nations —South Korea, Taiwan, Malaysia, and Singapore—are, together with the Chinese territory of Hong Kong, often known as the "Young Tigers." Their economies have grown rapidly in recent years to rival older industrial nations in manufacturing output and in technological resources and ability.

The economies of these nations' coasts were, like those of the islands, once based on ocean resources. Fishing and shipping are still part of the picture, but manufacturing industries now line shores along much of the Pacific Rim, employing millions of people.

Peru has one of the world's largest fishing fleets and some of the richest fishing grounds in its offshore waters. These fish are menhaden being processed at a Peruvian factory along the Pacific coast.

Harvesting the Ocean

The islands of Oceania and the islands and coasts of the far north and south, however, present a different picture. In Micronesia, Melanesia, and Polynesia, people continue to rely on the ocean for their resources. Many also depend on tourism. On the coasts of South America, in the Aleutian Islands, and in communities around the Bering Sea and the Sea of Okhotsk, people also harvest the ocean's resources. In the north, fishing and whaling provide food for small Native communities. The oil and gas industries are also important in remote northern areas.

Fishing

The commercial fishing grounds of the Pacific are among the world's most productive. Over half of the world's total catch of fish and shellfish are netted there. Eight out of ten of the largest fishing fleets are owned by nations bordering the Pacific: Japan, Russia, the United States, China, Peru, Chile, South Korea, and Indonesia. Commercial fishing is also carried out on a smaller scale by island nations.

The Northwest Pacific and shallows of the continental shelves are particularly rich in fish and shellfish. There, commercial fleets and local fishermen target tuna, salmon, pollack, herring, mackerel, sardines, anchovies, and shrimp.

South American Fishing Grounds

The coastal waters of Chile and Peru are among the world's richest fishing grounds because of the upwellings there. Small fish called anchoveta abound, providing a major source of food both for local people and other nations. Another local industry has also grown up based on the anchoveta—workers harvest the droppings of seabirds that feed on the fish. The droppings, known as guano, are sold as fertilizer. In El Niño years, however, the warmer water causes stocks of anchoveta to plummet. This drop causes hardship both for the marine food chain and for coastal fishing communities.

Other Ocean Industries

As well as fish and shellfish, the Pacific holds other live resources, including pearl oysters, corals, and seaweed. Reef fish are captured for the aquarium trade. **Aquaculture** is an important industry—

tuna, salmon, and shellfish are reared in pens and floating cages on the coasts of China, Japan, the United States, and elsewhere. Seaweed, a major food for Asian nations, is farmed in Japan.

Mineral Resources

Various parts of the Pacific are rich in minerals, including monazite, titanium, and platinum. Gold deposits are found

Pearls in the Pacific

Pearls, formed inside the shells of oysters, have been prized as gems for thousands of years. They can be all shapes and colors—white, round pearls are most often used in jewelry, but black pearls are especially valued for their rarity. Natural pearls are found off the coasts of Australia, Japan, Central America, and many Pacific islands. Pearls have tradition-ally been harvested by skilled divers, many of them women. Today, more pearls are harvested in pearl farms along Pacific coasts than in the wild.

When a pearl farmer plants a bead in an oyster shell, the oyster reacts by forming a pearl around it. The process can take two to four years, during which period oysters are kept in sheltered Pacific waters. Japan, Australia, the Cook Islands, and French Polynesia have thriving pearl industries, while the Solomon Islands and Fiji are establishing pearl farms to create jobs in coastal communities.

A diver in French Polynesia checks on the development of pearls at an oyster farm on the island of Marutea.

on the shores of Alaska, Fiji, and the Solomon Islands. Tin is mined off Southeast Asia, while titanium, chromium, and zircon are extracted off North American coasts. Iron ore is mined in the western Pacific. New Caledonia is the world's fourth-largest nickel producer. Phosphate mining is a major industry on the small islands of Nauru and Banaba.

Salt is extracted from seawater by evaporation, especially along the coast of Mexico. The United States, Japan, and other nations recover bromine and magnesium from their coastal waters. Sand, gravel, and even coral are **dredged** from the ocean bed for use in construction by the mainland United States, Hawaii, and Japan. The dredging process, however, can destroy natural habitats and cloud the water, which harms fish, shellfish, and reef-building corals.

The continental shelves of the Pacific Ocean hold large amounts of oil and natural gas, which are burned to provide energy. The offshore rigs of California, Alaska, China, Indonesia, and Australia

Australia's Gold Coast is popular with surfers and boaters. These competitors are lining up along the Gold Coast for a race.

are among the most productive in the region. Natural gas is mined off the coasts of Russia, Southeast Asia, and Australia.

Tourism

Tourism is a major industry in many parts of the Pacific. For some small island nations, tourism provides the main source of income. Millions of tourists fly to tropical Pacific coasts and islands each year to enjoy the climate and clear waters, the long beaches and coral reefs, and the varied cultures. Popular activities include surfing in Australia and Hawaii, sport fishing in Mexico, whale watching in Alaska and New Zealand, and diving and snorkeling around coral reefs and atolls. Hawaii and Australia's Gold Coast are among the most visited destinations. Cities such as San Francisco, Vancouver, Singapore, and Sydney are also major attractions.

CHAPTER SEVEN

ENVIRONMENT AND THE FUTURE

In the last half century, Pacific Ocean environments have begun to suffer from the rising numbers of people living on coasts and islands.

Changing Habitats

All around the Pacific, people have altered coastal habitats. Mangrove forests, an important marine habitat, have been cut down in many areas. Forests in North America and Southeast Asia have been extensively logged. The bare soil left behind washes into the sea, smothering coral reefs and the ocean bed. Mining has wrecked habitats on some coasts and islands. Phosphate mining has damaged much of Nauru and Banaba, while nickel mining has spoiled parts of New Caledonia. Mining has damaged coral reefs, too. The reefs are further harmed by divers who break off bits of coral and by fishermen dynamiting reef fish.

Coastal Pollution

Pollution is a threat in the Pacific Ocean, especially in coastal waters. Towns, farms, and factories on coasts and nearby rivers discharge waste of various kinds into the water. Towns release **sewage**, detergents, and other chemicals. Factories give off

Ninety percent of the tiny island of Nauru has become a wasteland as a result of phosphate mining. Nauru is home to more than twelve thousand people, and its economy has collapsed.

Workers used high pressure hot water to clean up oil after the 1989 Exxon Valdez *oil spill in Pacific waters off Alaska. Seabirds, otters, and countless fish and shellfish died because of the accident.*

poisonous wastes as byproducts of manufacturing, and these wastes are then absorbed by marine life.

Mercury absorbed by fish can reach levels dangerous to humans who consume the fish. In the 1950s, mercury from a factory at Minamata Bay in Japan was absorbed by local shellfish. More than six hundred people died after eating the shellfish. Today, mining and the burning of coal still contribute to mercury levels in the marine food chain.

Fertilizers used by farmers on land are washed into the sea and cause algae to multiply quickly in coastal waters. The increase in algae reduces oxygen levels in the water, which harms life in the ocean.

Deep Sea Dumping

The open waters of the Pacific are polluted by waste that has been deliberately or accidentally released. From the 1940s to the 1990s, radioactive waste from power plants and factories was dumped at sea. The ocean was thought to be big enough to absorb it—in fact, radioactive waste in the water cycle is hazardous to all life. In 1993, the practice was banned, but the nuclear waste already in the ocean will be radioactive for thousands of years.

Accidental oil spills have caused major pollution. In 1989, the oil tanker *Exxon Valdez* spilled 11 million gallons (42 million liters) of oil into the ocean after hitting a reef in Prince William Sound, Alaska. The oil polluted 1,200 miles (1,930 km) of coastline and killed up to half a million seabirds.

Nuclear Testing

Since the mid-1900s, some Pacific islands have been heavily contaminated by the testing of nuclear weapons by Britain, France, and the United States. In the 1950s and 1960s, the United States dropped a total of seventy nuclear bombs on the coral islands of Bikini and Enewetak, making them uninhabitable. The huge lagoon of Kwajalein in the Marshall Islands was used as a target for missiles from the U.S. mainland. France has exploded more than eighty nuclear bombs on Mururoa in Polynesia. In each case, the islands' inhabitants were removed. High levels of radiation may remain, making it unsafe for people to return. In the 1990s, the French resumed nuclear tests on Mururoa despite worldwide protests.

Many Pacific nations are now taking action to curb environmental threats. In 1982, the United Nations drafted the Law of the Sea treaty, which restricts pollution and regulates fishing and mining. The treaty came into effect in 1994.

Overfishing

The practice of **overfishing** by commercial fishing fleets threatens stocks of Pacific shellfish and fish, including halibut, anchovies, king crab, perch, and salmon. Such high numbers of these species have been caught that not enough are left to breed. Other creatures are trapped and drowned in fishing nets, and their bodies are just dumped at sea. Fishing authorities can impose restrictions on the fishing industry to combat these problems. Aquaculture can also help ease pressure on the wild stocks.

Endangered Species

Across the Pacific, some species of reptiles, birds, and mammals—including sea otters, dugongs, and sea lions—are threatened by hunting. Guadalupe fur seals, for example, and several types of sea turtles are now scarce because so many have been killed for their meat, fur, or shells.

Unique species on Pacific islands are put at risk when people introduce new types of animals to their islands. Sheep

Turtle Crisis

"Throughout Asia and the Americas, Pacific leatherback populations are disappearing. This is a flagship crisis in marine **biodiversity**, and if we don't listen to the message in the rapid decline of leatherback populations, other large pelagic migratory species will be next . . . with dire consequences for the marine environment."

Wallace J. Nichols, director of U.S.-based conservation project Wildcoast, 2002

and goats can destroy island vegetation. The island of Guam has been overrun by snakes, accidentally brought by humans, and the snakes threaten native wildlife. Endangered Pacific birds include the honeycreeper birds of Hawaii, Humboldt penguins, and several flightless birds of New Zealand, such as the takahe.

Conservation Efforts

Conservationists have protected the takahe by releasing it on the islands of Kapiti, Mana, Tiritiri Matangi, and Maud, where it has no predators. The tuatara is a unique reptile that has been protected in a similar fashion. The most effective way of helping wild species is to protect their whole environment by setting up marine parks and nature reserves. Australia's Great Barrier Reef and Monterey Bay, California, are two examples of such marine reserves.

The Future of the Pacific Ocean

The future of the Pacific Ocean will involve rapid development as more people and industries move to coastal areas. The demands of people and industry will have an increasing impact. The key to dealing with this demand is sustainable development—finding ways of using the Pacific's resources and living on its coasts while protecting the environment for future generations.

Science helps in facing the challenges of the future. New forms of energy are being developed that may be able to use Pacific Ocean resources without causing pollution or harming marine life. These include harnessing the energy of tides and waves as well as using the ocean's vast supply of thermal energy, or heat, to generate elecrical power. Scientists in the Pacific are even exploring ways to

The Tiritiri Matangi Island Open Sanctuary is home to the takahe, a bird that used to be widespread in New Zealand.

reduce global warming by using the ocean's natural ability to absorb carbon dioxide. New systems to predict the world's changing climate patterns may help Pacific coastal and island communities face the challenges of the future.

Global Warming

A climate change identified in the last few years is affecting the world's oceans. World temperatures are slowly but steadily rising, partly because of air pollution from the burning of **fossil fuels**. Gases given off when these fuels burn trap the Sun's heat to produce warmer weather. The rising temperatures are warming the oceans, which makes the water expand and so raises sea levels. There are signs that land ice in polar regions may melt into the oceans because of warmer temperatures, and this would dramatically raise sea levels. Low-lying cities, such as Tokyo and Sydney, could flood. Small island nations, such as Kiribati, could disappear altogether. Scientists believe that global warming will bring more storms and El Niño events. Warmer water also harms coral reefs. Many nations around the world, however, are making an effort to address global warming by reducing energy consumption and cutting down on air pollution.

TIME LINE

About 90,000 B.C. Pacific shores of eastern Asia are inhabited by humans.

About 50,000 B.C. Humans move south from eastern Asia to settle Indonesia, New Guinea, and Australia.

By 15,000 B.C. Humans reach the Americas from Asia and spread to inhabit all areas.

2,000 B.C. Groups from Southeast Asia sail east to live on islands in the Pacific Ocean.

By A.D. 500 Islands of eastern Polynesia are inhabited.

By A.D. 800 Polynesians reach New Zealand.

1500s–1700s European powers claim territories on many coasts bordering the Pacific Ocean.

1520–1521 Portuguese navigator Ferdinand Magellan sails across the Pacific Ocean.

1606 Dutch explorer Willem Jansz is the first European to reach Australia.

1642 Dutch explorer Abel Tasman visits New Zealand.

1768–1769 British explorer James Cook makes several voyages in the Pacific and charts many new islands.

1835 British naturalist Charles Darwin visits Galápagos Islands in the eastern Pacific and develops theory of evolution partly based on observations there.

1849 California Gold Rush begins.

1874–1875 British research ship HMS *Challenger* makes the first scientific study of ocean depths, including the Pacific Ocean.

1907 Australia and New Zealand gain independence from the United Kingdom.

1914 Panama Canal opens, providing a shortcut between the Pacific and Atlantic Oceans.

1930–1942 Japanese forces occupy many islands in Pacific Ocean.

1941 Japanese attack on Pearl Harbor, Hawaii, draws United States into World War II.

1945 United States drops atomic bombs on Hiroshima and Nagasaki.

1950s–1960s France, Britain, and the United States conduct nuclear bomb tests in the Pacific Ocean.

1950s-1980s Rapid industrialization in Japan is followed by industrialization in other Pacific Rim nations.

1959 Hawaii becomes the fiftieth U.S. state.

1960 Swiss scientist Jacques Piccard and Don Walsh of the U.S. Navy descend to Challenger Deep in the submersible *Trieste*.

1977 First hydrothermal vents are discovered, at the Galápagos Ridge.

1989 Oil tanker *Exxon Valdez* causes major oil spill after hitting a reef in Prince William Sound, Alaska.

1994 Law of the Sea treaty to curb pollution and control fishing and mining comes into effect.

1995 France resumes nuclear tests in Pacific Ocean despite widespread protests.

1996 Japanese unmanned submersible *Kaiko* explores Challenger Deep.

GLOSSARY

abyssal zone ocean below 6,600 feet (2,000 m)

algae tiny, simple plants or plant-like organisms that grow in water or damp places

aquaculture farming of marine species—such as fish, pearl oysters, or mussels—in ocean water or inland waters

barrier island island lying parallel to the shore that protects mainland from the open ocean

bathyal zone mid-depths of ocean water between 330–660 feet deep and 6,600 feet deep (100–200 m deep and 2,000 m deep)

biodiversity variety of life in a habitat; greater diversity increases the ability of life forms to evolve and adapt to environmental changes

cape point of land that juts out into water

colony territory claimed by a nation or area occupied by settlers

condense change from gas into liquid

container large crate—used on ships, trains, and trucks—that combines many smaller pieces of freight into one shipment for efficient loading and unloading

continental drift theory that landmasses are not fixed but slowly drift across Earth's surface because of tectonic plate movement

current regular flow of water in a certain direction

delta land composed of mud and sand deposited around the mouth of a river

dredge gather by scooping up or digging out

equator imaginary line around the middle of Earth lying an equal distance between the North Pole and South Pole

euphotic zone upper layer of ocean water, usually defined as above 330–660 feet (100–200 m)

evaporate turn from liquid into gas

evolve change and adapt over a long period of time

fossil fuel coal, oil, natural gas, and other fuels formed in the ground from remains of plants or animals

freight cargo transported by sea, air, rail, or road

gulf large inlet of an ocean

gyre surface current in an ocean or sea that moves in a clockwise or counterclockwise circle

habitat type of place, such as a mountain or coral reef, where plants and animals live

hull body of a ship. Some vessels have two hulls, joined by a deck or other structure, for stability.

isthmus narrow strip of land connecting two larger landmasses

lagoon shallow area of water near a larger body of water

latitude distance north or south of the equator

lava hot, melted rock on Earth's surface that has welled up from under the ground

longitude distance east or west of the prime meridian

low pressure atmospheric system that produces unstable, stormy weather. (High pressure produces stable weather with clear skies.) Air pressure is the weight of the atmosphere pressing down on Earth at any given point.

magma molten rock beneath the surface of Earth

mantle part of Earth between the crust and the core. It is mostly solid rock, but part of it is molten.

migrate move from one place to another

mollusk group of animals with thin, sometimes soft shells, including clams, squid, octopus, and snails

navigation use of animal instinct or scientific skills to determine a route or steer a course on a journey

outrigger framework attached to the side of a canoe to support a float that gives the boat stability

overfishing catching so many fish that stocks are depleted or species made extinct

peninsula piece of land jutting out into water but connected to mainland

photosynthesis process in which plants use carbon dioxide, hydrogen, and light to produce their food

plankton microscopic plants (phytoplankton) and animals (zooplankton) that float at the surface of oceans and lakes and provide food for many larger animals

polyp small sea animal with tube-like body and tentacles that attaches to rock or other substance

prevailing wind main wind in a particular region

radar system that detects and locates objects by bouncing radio waves off them

reef chain of rock or coral or raised strip of sand in water

ridge raised area on land or on ocean bottom

rift opening on land or in the ocean where the ground has split apart

salinity level of salt in water

salvage saving or recovering of objects, such as treasure from a shipwreck

satellite vehicle that orbits Earth that can be used to send signals to Earth for communications systems; or any object in space that orbits another, larger object

sediment loose particles of rocky material, such as sand or mud

sewage dirty water from homes and factories containing chemicals and human waste

shingle deposit of small rocks, like large gravel, usually found on coastlines

shoal bank of sand just below the water surface in an ocean or sea

sonar (short for sound navigation and ranging) system that uses sound waves to measure ocean depth and detect and locate underwater objects

spit long, narrow finger of land stretching out into water

strait water channel that connects two areas of water

subduction zone region where two tectonic plates press together, causing one to subduct, or dive below the other

submersible small underwater craft often used to explore deep parts of the ocean

subtropical in or having to do with the region of the world that borders the Tropics

tanker ship fitted with tanks for carrying liquid

tropical in or having to do with the region of the world known as the Tropics

Tropics region of the world either side of the equator between the tropic of Cancer and the tropic of Capricorn

upwelling periodic rise of dense, cold water to the ocean's surface when warmer surface waters are pulled away by currents

FURTHER RESOURCES

Books

Innes, Brian. *Down to a Sunless Sea: The Strange World of Hydrothermal Vents.* Sagebrush, 2000.

Mallory, Kenneth. *Swimming with Hammerhead Sharks.* Scientists in the Field (series). Houghton Mifflin, 2001.

Matsen, Brad. *The Incredible Submersible* Alvin *Discovers a Strange Deep-Sea World.* Incredible Deep-Sea Adventures (series). Enslow Publishers, 2003.

Rhodes, Mary Jo. *Octopuses and Squids.* Undersea Encounters (series). Children's Press, 2005.

White, David. *The First Voyage Around the World: The Story of Ferdinand Magellan's Three-Year Journey Through South America and the Pacific Ocean.* Exploration and Discovery (series). Mason Crest, 2002.

Williams, Jean Kinney. *Cook: James Cook Charts the Pacific Ocean.* Exploring the World (series). Compass Point Books, 2003.

Woodward, John. *Midnight Zone.* Exploring the Oceans (series). Heinemann, 2004.

Web Sites

Defenders of Wildlife—Marine
www.defenders.org/wildlife/new/marine.html

JASON—Lost City Hydrothermal Vents—Kids' Corner
lostcity.jason.org/kids_corner.aspx

NOAA Ocean Explorer: Galapagos Rift
oceanexplorer.noaa.gov/explorations/02galapagos/galapagos.html

Reef Education Network
www.reef.edu.au/

The Space Place: MISR Watches Tsunami
spaceplace.nasa.gov/en/kids/misr_tsunami/index.shtml

Volcanoes, Earthquakes, Hurricanes, Tornadoes
www.nationalgeographic.com/forcesofnature/interactive/

About the Author

Jen Green worked in publishing for fifteen years. She is now a full-time author and has written more than 150 books for children about natural history, geography, the environment, history, and other topics.

INDEX

5/06

mL